THE POWER OF A PROMISE

by Charles R. Swindoll

ZondervanPublishingHouse

Grand Rapids, Michigan

A Division of HarperCollinsPublishers

The Power of a Promise

Copyright © 1994 by Charles R. Swindoll, Inc.

Requests for information should be addressed to:

Zondervan Publishing House
5300 Patterson Avenue S.E.
Grand Rapids, Michigan 49530

ISBN 0-310-48762-5

■ Printed in the United States of America

■ Cover Design by: DesignTeam, Brian L. Fowler

94 95 96 97 98 / LP / 5 4 3 2 1

THE POWER OF A PROMISE

The power of a promise is incredible!

It is impossible to overestimate the impact a promise can make on us and on those to whom we make that promise. Sometimes it is so powerful, so meaningful, a person is able to survive on nothing more than the strength a promise provides.

In 1989 an 8.2 earthquake almost flattened Armenia, killing over 30,000 people in less than four minutes.

In the midst of utter devastation and chaos, a father left his wife securely at home and rushed to the school where his son was supposed to be, only to discover that the building was as flat as a pancake.

After the traumatic initial shock, he remembered the promise he had made to his son: "No matter what, I'll always be there for you!" And tears began to fill his eyes. As he looked at the pile of debris that once was the school, it looked hopeless, but he kept remembering his commitment to his son.

He began to concentrate on where he walked his son to class at school each morning. Remembering his son's classroom would be in the back right corner of the building, he rushed there and started digging through the rubble.

As he was digging, other forlorn parents arrived, clutching their hearts, saying: "My son!" "My daughter!" Other well meaning parents tried to pull him off of what was left of the school, saying:

"It's too late!"

"They're dead!"

"You can't help!"

"Go home!"

"Come on, face reality, there's nothing you can do!"

"You're just going to make things worse!"

To each parent he responded with one line: "Are you going to help me now?" And then he proceeded to dig for his son, stone by stone.

The fire chief showed up and tried to pull him off of the school's debris, saying, "Fires are breaking out, explosions are happening everywhere.

You're in danger. We'll take care of it. Go home." To which this loving, caring Armenian father asked, "Are you going to help me now?"

The police came and said, "You're angry, distraught, and it's over. You're endangering others. Go home. We'll handle it!" To which he replied, "Are you going to help me now?" No one helped.

Courageously he proceeded alone because he needed to know for himself: "Is my boy alive or is he dead?"

He dug for eight hours . . . twelve hours . . . twenty-four hours . . . thirty-six hours . . . then, in the thirty-eighth hour, he pulled back a boulder and heard his son's voice. He screamed his son's name, "*ARMAND!*" He heard back, "Dad!?! It's me, Dad! I told the other kids not to worry. I told 'em that if you were alive, you'd save me and when you saved me, they'd be saved. You promised: 'No matter what, I'll always be there for you!' You did it, Dad!"

"What's going on in there? How is it?" the father asked.

"There are fourteen of us left out of thirty-three, Dad. We're scared, hungry, thirsty and thankful you're here. When the building collapsed, it made a wedge, like a triangle, and it saved us."

"Come on out, boy!"

"No, Dad! Let the other kids out first, 'cause I know you'll get me! No matter what, I know you'll be there for me!"[1]

The power of a promise is incredible!

You and I may never be called upon to endure an experience anywhere near that dramatic, but that doesn't diminish the importance of making a promise and going the full extent to keep it.

A promise is a commitment, a pledge . . . a verbal and/or written declaration that we will do (or refrain from doing) something. To those to whom we make our promise, it becomes a reason to expect something from us. That expectation brings confidence, reassurance, and courage.

Armand's father made a promise, a stated commitment, that reassured the lad that his dad would "always be there" for him. Those few words became Armand's lifeline . . . literally. Not even being buried alive in a tiny space beneath tons of debris for almost two full days could erase that father's promise from his son's mind.

When was the last time you went on record and made a commitment regarding someone in your family? I'm not referring merely to thinking about them or praying for them, important though those things may be. I have in mind a definite statement, a well-thought-through pledge to one or more persons to whom you are related. We could broaden the scope to include others in our sphere of influence, but limiting our thoughts to the family, we will be able to fine-tune our focus.

FAMILY PROMISES: THREE CATEGORIES

Rather than enlarging the base of family promises so far that we dilute their impact, let's concentrate our attention on three specific relationships:

1. *Our relationships with those who have gone before us—our mom and/or dad.*

2. *Our relationships with those who are going along with us—our husband or wife.*

3. *Our relationships with those who will come after us—our children.*

Clearly, these are the ones to whom we are most closely tied and have known the best. Yet, isn't it interesting, they are also the ones we tend to take for granted . . . to assume they are fully convinced of our commitment. It would surprise you to know how seldom those things are true. Parents and mates and children, more often than not, need the reassurance that only our promise can provide. When we take the time to think it through and then communicate our commitment to those who fall into those three categories, it is amazing what a difference it can make.

Let's pause and consider first the importance of our promise to our mother and/or our father.

"MOM AND DAD, I PROMISE . . . "

According to the Scriptures, the relationship we sustain with our parents is to be one of *honor* and *respect*.

Read the following Bible verses slowly and thoughtfully:

> Honor your father and your mother, that your days may be prolonged in the land which the LORD your God gives you.
>
> Exodus 20:12

> Every one of you shall reverence his mother and his father. . . .
>
> Leviticus 19:3

> Honor your father and your mother, as the LORD your God has commanded you, that your days may be prolonged, and that it may go well with you in the land which the LORD your God gives you.
>
> Deuteronomy 5:16

> HONOR YOUR FATHER AND MOTHER (which is the first commandment with a promise), THAT IT MAY BE WELL WITH YOU, AND THAT YOU MAY LIVE LONG ON THE EARTH.
>
> Ephesians 6:2-3

As you look back over those state-
ments from the Scriptures, you will
observe that they are not suggestions or
some kind of multiple-choice alternatives;
they are *commands*. Whenever we come
across biblical commands, the appropriate response is to obey. We may analyze,
discuss, probe into their meaning, and
ponder the implications . . . but the bot-
tom line of a command is clear: We are to
do *exactly* what the Lord requires. And
in this case? We are to give honor and
show respect to our parents.

We may be tempted to rationalize our
way out of this responsibility or ignore it
altogether. To do so would be in step with
our times, where parents have become the
scapegoats in our blaming society.
Perhaps you have reason to criticize your
mom or dad; one or both of them may
have taken unfair advantage of you or
neglected you when you really needed
them to be there for you. They may not
have protected you or provided for you
when you were young and vulnerable.

If you are like most, rather than for-
giving them and being big enough to see
beyond the pain and the scars, you have
taken either the passive route and decided to ignore them . . . or you have chosen
the aggressive response and bitterly
blamed them—maybe you have written
them off altogether. It may surprise you

to read that I understand; I could easily have done either, in light of the things I experienced as an unwanted child. The favoritism shown to my older brother (by my mother) and my older sister (by my father) was obvious to me. I can still hear my mom's words to me: "You were a mistake." They hurt. The pain occasionally surfaces even though I am sixty years of age and certainly should be able to get past it.

Even more vivid in my memory is the day I chose to forgive them. It was a deliberate and sincere choice, especially significant since the alternative was taking a toll on me emotionally. What's worse, I found that as long as I was caught in the grip of an unforgiving spirit, there was no way I could obey God's command. Honor and respect would not flow from my unforgiving heart. What's true of me is equally true of you. You may find it necessary to deal with *that* issue before you can come to terms with *this* one. If so, I strongly encourage you to do it.

In a fine book, *The Tribute*, on the importance of honoring our parents, Dennis Rainey calls this scriptural imperative the "forgotten command." With appropriate passion Rainey writes:

> . . . Instead of honoring our parents, we've taken the better part of the past three decades to bash, blame, and attack our parents for their faults

and failures. Our parents have become a toxic waste site on which to dump the blame of our dysfunction. In the process of analyzing our backgrounds—which I believe is indeed an important part of growing up—we have failed to take responsibility for our own attitudes and actions. We have failed to obey that which God clearly commands: to honor our parents.[2]

Let me cut to the chase rather than get bogged down in the swamp of self-pity, blame, or anger. You and I, in order to obey what God has commanded, must *forgive the failures of our parents*. I urge you, do that sooner rather than later—preferably *right now!* Work that out with the Lord (and, if necessary, those who can help you get beyond the snags), then begin to think about affirming your promise to "honor your father and mother." Please keep in mind that this particular command includes God's promise to you: It "will be well with you" (your quality of life will be enhanced) and you "may live long on the earth" (your length of life could very well be extended).

Those two benefits are God's rewards to all who commit themselves to honoring and respecting their parents. Will you be one of them? I hope so! Your verbal pledge can become the beginning of a whole new relationship.

Remember, the power of a promise is incredible!

"SWEETHEART, I PROMISE . . . "

There is a second relationship that calls for our commitment. I'm referring to the relationship we sustain with our married partner. I know, I know, you've already taken your vows; isn't that enough? Well, it's enough to make your marriage legal, but I have found that those original vows are not enough to keep the husband-wife union strong and harmonious. Strong marriages don't "just happen" any more than a car automatically stays in good running condition or a garden remains productive and free of weeds. Maintenance is essential. Furthermore, when a marriage is properly maintained, promises must be made and kept. The key words are *love* and *acceptance*.

Let's go back to the Scriptures and reexamine God's original design for a husband and wife.

> The LORD God said, "It is not good for the man to be alone; I will make him a helper suitable for him." And out of the ground the LORD God formed every beast of the field and

every bird of the sky, and brought
them to the man to see what he would
call them; and whatever the man
called a living creature, that was its
name. And the man gave names to all
the cattle, and to the birds of the sky,
and to every beast of the field, but for
Adam there was not found a helper
suitable for him. So the LORD God
caused a deep sleep to fall upon the
man, and he slept; then He took one of
his ribs, and closed up the flesh at that
place. And the LORD God fashioned
into a woman the rib which He had
taken from the man, and brought her
to the man. . . .

For this cause a man shall leave
his father and his mother, and shall
cleave to his wife; and they shall
become one flesh. And the man and
his wife were both naked and were not
ashamed.

Genesis 2:18-22, 24-25

A closer look at those words uncovers
no less than four all-important guidelines
for a harmonious marriage:

1. Severance	*". . . shall leave father and mother"*	
2. Permanence	*". . . shall cleave"*	
3. Unity	*". . . one flesh"*	
4. Intimacy	*"naked . . . not ashamed."*	

This is a good time to ask yourself several hard questions:

- *Have I really severed my ties with Mom and Dad?*
- *Am I truly and permanently bonded with my mate?*
- *Is there a unity between us? Are we pulling together or apart?*
- *Have I done my part to cultivate intimacy with my mate? If not, why not?*

Solomon, in his book of wisdom, the Proverbs, offers several helpful hints to husbands and wives.

Let your fountain be blessed,
And rejoice in the wife of your youth.
As a loving hind and a graceful doe,
Let her breasts satisfy you at all times;
Be exhilarated always with her love.
For why should you, my son, be exhil-
     arated with an adulteress,
And embrace the bosom of a foreigner?
For the ways of a man are before the
     eyes of the LORD,
And He watches all his paths.
                      Proverbs 5:18-21

An excellent wife is the crown of her
     husband,
But she who shames him is as rotten-
     ness in his bones.
                      Proverbs 12:4

He who finds a wife finds a good thing,

And obtains favor from the LORD.

Proverbs 18:22

House and wealth are an inheritance
from fathers,
But a prudent wife is from the LORD.

Proverbs 19:14

An excellent wife, who can find?
For her worth is far above jewels.

Proverbs 31:10

What great words to ponder!

And we dare not overlook Paul's timeless advice:

> Wives, be subject to your own husbands, as to the Lord. For the husband is the head of the wife, as Christ also is the head of the church, He Himself being the Savior of the body. But as the church is subject to Christ, so also the wives ought to be to their husbands in everything. Husbands, love your wives, just as Christ also loved the church and gave Himself up for her.
>
> Ephesians 5:22-25

Talk about convicting! As a wife, is your love for your man so deep, so strong, that you are willing to *live* for him? As a husband, is your love for the woman God gave you so profound that you are willing to *die* for her? And how about your acceptance of each other? Are you working overtime, trying hard to change your mate . . . or are you willing to look him or her in the eyes and promise to love and accept your partner even if nothing changes?

When I think of love, four thoughts come to my mind, each tied in with the word itself:

1. L . . . *when I love my partner, I listen when she speaks; I hear her advice, I heed her warnings, I respect her concerns. She speaks . . . I listen.*

2. O . . . *those who love—truly love—their partners overlook a lot of things—little idiosyncrasies, petty differences, words said in irritable moments, etc.*

3. V . . . *love and acceptance means we value our partner. We say so! We value his or her opinions, tastes, choices, warnings, and needs. We treat such people with courtesy and kindness.*

4. E . . . *love is displayed, it is expressed. Love and acceptance are not just hidden feelings, they are translated into actions—not merely inclinations, but demonstrations.*

A major enemy in any home is selfishness . . . and in a marriage, that often expresses itself in jealousy. Again, I know what I'm talking about! There was a time in my own life when jealousy ate away at me like a cancer. In fact, it almost ruined my relationship with my wife, Cynthia.

Let me relate a true story that illustrates how the Lord was at work in me, determined to rid me of this major character weakness. It's a little humorous now . . . but back when this happened, it seemed as serious as a heart attack.

Cynthia and I lived in Texas when we first met. She and I dated only a week before I asked her to marry me. She said yes . . . but she added that she had a date the next day and she didn't feel right about breaking it off. (She felt she should keep her promise!) I struggled with her decision. Remember now, I was the jealous type. So the idea of her being with anyone other than me was unthinkable.

To make matters worse, she was going to a Texas A & M football game with one of the Aggie cadets. "Horrible," it seemed to me; not only because he was an Aggie(!), but also because the Texas Aggies had a tradition that every time they made a touchdown, the cadet kissed his date!

All this transpired in the early 1950s. My only relief was that back then A & M rarely scored a touchdown! My great hope was that they would be shut out.

I was glued to the radio the next day,

consumed with anxiety and jealousy. All I could picture was my wife-to-be in the arms of another man. Guess what happened? Texas A & M won 48-0! That's a lot of kisses, friend. God has His ways of dealing with us, doesn't He?

Is there something that is standing in the way of your love, your acceptance of your marriage partner? I had to come to terms with my jealousy. It was an extremely painful struggle, but (thank the Lord!) He enabled me to face it, to realize how it stemmed from my own insecurities, and to overcome it. It took quite some time for me to overcome that long-standing weakness. Finally, I was able to get beyond it. I can honestly say, a thought of jealousy rarely, if ever, crosses my mind today. What a wonderful relief!

I repeat, is there something you need to deal with that is hindering the harmony of your marriage? Some selfish habit? How about your temper? Or perhaps your unwillingness to flex and change? Maybe you are trying to make your spouse into someone else . . . or you are making demands that he/she cannot meet. If so, do you realize what a wedge this is driving between the two of you?

It's time for a change! You probably are not ready to face the fact that your unattractive habit or resistance is eroding your partner's affection. I need to warn you that if it continues, it may very well ruin what was once a beautiful and promising marriage.

It's time for you to think through the words of a promise regarding your love for and acceptance of your mate. Those words will do no good if they stay in your mind; they need to be stated. As I said earlier, love is demonstrative . . . something we express. Who knows what a difference your words can make?

I repeat, the power of a promise is incredible!

"MY SON, MY DAUGHTER, I PROMISE . . . "

Now we have come to the "clincher." I don't know of a more important promise we can make regarding the future than the one(s) we make to our children. When I think about a parent's relationship with his or her children, two words come to mind: *nurturing* and *modeling*.

Both of those words grow out of the same section of Scripture:

> And, fathers, do not provoke your children to anger; but bring them up in the discipline and instruction of the Lord.
>
> Ephesians 6:4

Even a quick glance at those inspired words reveals that a negative command

precedes a positive one. Equally significant, the negative is specifically connected
to "fathers." We who are fathers must
admit that we are usually the ones who
provoke our children to anger.

In Colossians 3:21, similar words
appear:

> Fathers, do not exasperate your
> children, that they may not lose heart.

The New International Version ren-
ders this:

> Father, do not embitter your chil-
> dren, or they will become discour-
> aged.

Let's face it, more often than not,
mothers have a kind of "divine patience,"
a built-in understanding of their children.
I have found that dads, more often than
not, must deliberately cultivate those
qualities.

The plague of the father-child relationship, I have observed, is creating a
broken spirit in a child's life. How? A
child becomes demoralized and discour-
aged by the father's almost continual
stream of criticism, harsh words, stinging
rebukes . . . which frequently leads to dis-
cipline that is administered too often, too
quickly, too severely.

Mothers can fall into the same trap, I

realize, but this seems to be a special weakness among dads. We men are usually much more demanding. We love our children, but we rarely express enough affirmation and encouragement. We have too many expectations and are too controlling.

So much for the negative—the problem.

Look at the bright side—the solution.

We, the parents, are to "bring them up" differently. Originally, those three English words came from one Greek term (used only here and in Ephesians 4:29) that means "to nurture, to nourish." It's a beautiful word . . . rich with meaning. Hidden within the first-century term is understanding, emotion, caring, time, and attention. Picture the parent—

- *who pays attention when attention is needed,*
- *who protects when protection is needed,*
- *who encourages when encouragement is needed,*
- *who gives wise counsel when counsel is needed,*
- *who knows what's going on in and around the life of a son or daughter.*

In other words, when a parent "nurtures" a child, the needs of the child become a priority. The by-product of that is this: We leave the right impression on the life of our child. Our investment yields lingering dividends.

I love the word picture Randy Carlson uses as he describes this in his excellent work, *Father Memories:*

> Fathers leave a lasting impression on the lives of their children. Picture fathers all around the world carving their initials into their family trees. Like a carving in the trunk of an oak, as time passes the impressions fathers make on their children grow deeper and wider. Depending upon how the tree grows, those impressions can either be ones of harmony or ones of distortion.
>
> Some fathers skillfully carve beautiful messages of love, support, solid discipline, and acceptance into the personality core of their children. Others use words and actions that cut deeply and leave emotional scars. Time may heal the wound and dull the image, but the impression can never be completely erased. The size, shape, and extent of your father's imprint on your life may be large or may be small but it is undeniably there.[3]

This is a good time, moms and dads, to sit quietly, close your eyes, and push the replay button on the memory video inside your head. What scenes emerge?

- *Emotional reassurance and security?*
- *A strong moral and ethical value system?*
- *Healthy, wholesome, and needed boundaries?*
- *The importance of having fun, enjoying laughter?*
- *Cultivating a desire for an authentic spiritual life?*

So much of what our children become stems from the nurturing they receive and the modeling they witness in us as parents. How great is our need these days for keen-thinking, well-balanced, strong-hearted fathers and mothers! Why? Because they release to society similar kinds of offspring. Our times are marked by violence, compromise, sloppy thinking, and virtual absence of moral absolutes—not to mention an obvious spiritual decline. We face (in my opinion) a second "Reconstruction Period" as a nation, not unlike the years following the bloody Civil War.

In those days—a dark and dreadful era in American history—there was a desperate need for men. So many had been killed in the war. Our country needed stouthearted, clear-minded men in the

city, in state affairs, in the Oval Office.
Today we need men *and women* in those
places, young and middle-aged adults who
have character, who model integrity.

Josiah Holland wrote his piece,
"God, Give Us Men!" toward the end of
the nineteenth century, but it fits perfect-
ly one hundred years later:

GOD, GIVE US MEN! A time like
    this demands
Strong minds, great hearts, true
    faith and ready hands;
Men whom the lust of office does
    not kill;
Men whom the spoils of office can
    not buy;
Men who possess opinions and a
    will;
Men who have honor; men who will
    not lie;
Men who can stand before a dema-
    gogue
    And damn his treacherous flat-
    teries without winking!
Tall men, sun-crowned, who live
    above the fog
    In public duty and in private
    thinking;
For while the rabble, with their
    thumb-worn creeds,
Their large professions and their
    little deeds,

Mingle in selfish strife, lo! Freedom
weeps,
Wrong rules the land and waiting
Justice sleeps.[4]

As I read that poetic prayer recently,
it occurred to me that God does not suddenly give us men and women like that . . .
rather He gives little boys and little girls
to parents, very human and imperfect
men and women like you and me. These
little people are left under our protective
wings only a few years, and during that
time we have the awesome privilege as
well as the exacting responsibility to grow
them into men and women of God. In this
modern "Reconstruction Period," the
need is even greater now than it was back
then.

It won't happen unless we, the parents, are fully committed to nurturing
and to modeling. I suggest it's time for us
to make a third promise, this one to our
children. Believe me, it will not only
change *our* lives . . . but, far more importantly, it can change *theirs*. Chances are
good, if we don't declare a promise, no
change will occur.

IT'S TIME TO MAKE THREE PROMISES

We're back where we started: The
power of a promise is incredible! It is

impossible to overstate the impact a promise can make on us and on those to whom we make that promise.

There is no better time for doing the right thing than now. I have discovered in my six decades on this earth that putting off until later something I should take care of now is always wrong . . . always a regrettable decision.

Let's not do that. These things I have mentioned in this booklet are too important to put off any longer. How wise it would be for you to take care of these things today!

A BRIEF REVIEW

I have written about three vital commitments for a healthy family. These commitments call for an honest facing of the facts, then a careful wording of the promises, followed by a firm determination to do what ought to be done—both now and in the months and years to come.

We have considered our relationship with our parents, with our mates, and with our children. Let me urge you to concentrate only on those three specific realms of responsibility. In each one, I challenge you to be honest, sincere, and courageous.

PROMISES, PROMISES

Regarding Your Parents . . .

It may be that your area of greatest
need is here. In all honestly, this relationship may have been broken down for
years . . . or you may have a sort of
"unspoken" relationship because you've
never verbalized your commitment to
those who reared you. If this is true, here
is a promise—your vow before God—that
can make a definite difference. Repeat it
orally, only if you can do so with your
whole heart.

> *Lord, I promise to find a way to
> show honor and respect to my mother
> and father.*

Regarding Your Mate . . .

It is possible your greatest need lies
here, with the one to whom you are married. If so, I urge you to face that square-
ly and plan to confront it directly.
Marital erosion need not be terminal, but
it will take a power that is superhuman to
turn things around. That's why we are
calling on the living Lord as we declare
each of these promises. Here is a suggest-
ed promise that, if made and maintained,
could be the catalyst needed to bring the
two of you back together in a new and
fresh way. After reading it, consider stat-
ing these words aloud and alone before
God:

> *Lord, I promise to cultivate a relationship with my marriage partner based on love and acceptance.*

Regarding Your Children . . .

Quite probably, this third category is the one most universally in need of attention—our relationship with our children. All over the world children are desperately in need of (and often crying out for) their parents' time and attention as well as affection and correction. Yours may be among them. If so, you need to realize that solving the problem that has been in existence will be neither easy nor quick. But it isn't impossible! Your promise to begin anew could be the turning point. Again, read these words slowly and thoughtfully. If they reflect the truth, repeat them to the Lord today:

> *Lord, I promise to begin a relationship with my son/daughter where I will nurture him/her and model strong Christian character for the rest of my life.*

CONCLUSION

Two thoughts come to my mind as I bring this booklet to a close. One is a warning; the other, a memory.

The Scriptures clearly state the seriousness of taking a vow, which is the bib-

lical term for making a promise. Read
the warning carefully:

> When you make a vow to God, do
> not be late in paying it, for He takes
> no delight in fools. Pay what you vow!
> It is better that you should not vow
> than that you should vow and not pay.
>
> Ecclesiastes 5:4-5

In today's terms, that's saying don't
play games with God. Understand that
when we make a promise we should
remember that He doesn't mess around.
He hears us, He stands ready to assist us,
and He never forgets our words. He isn't
interested merely in promise-*making*, but
in promise-*keeping*. Few things are more
serious to God than a promise.

That prompts me to mention the
memory I referred to earlier. It was late
in May of 1994. I was invited to speak to
a gathering of men sponsored by
PromiseKeepers. The whole event lasted
two days; I was there for most of the time.
The place was Anaheim Stadium in
Southern California. Over 52,000 men
attended. My subject was "A Man and
His Family."

For almost forty minutes I had the
privilege of bringing the thoughts I have
written in this booklet to those men the
last evening we were together. What an

experience! You would have had to have been there to know fully what I mean when I use the word "electrifying." God's Spirit was among us. By His grace, the Lord anointed those minutes with His presence and His power. I had never spoken in a setting quite like that one and never before to a crowd that large.

As I reached the end of a passionate and very emotional delivery of the message, I didn't want to rely on the flesh or play on the highly charged emotions of the moment. I decided to ask the men simply to bow their heads and to sit quietly as I reviewed the same three important promises we've covered in this booklet.

The stadium became strangely silent, though packed with more than 50,000 men. I quietly asked the Lord for wisdom—for His leadership—as I concluded my presentation. How wonderfully He led!

I asked the men *not* to stand unless they meant business with God . . . and unless the particular promise applied to them personally. At that point I went to the first category regarding the showing of honor and respect for parents. Many stood . . . not all. I gave them the words to use and asked them to repeat after me. The sound was like rolling thunder as thousands of men promised to address their need to be sons who honored and respected their parents. Following the promise, silence returned.

We then went to the second category as I invited those who felt their marriage was in need of attention to stand. More stood, all over the stadium. God gripped my heart with the realization that beginning that cool evening in May, thousands upon thousands of marriages would begin to be restored.

Again, like a low rumble of continuous thunder, those masculine voices from bowed heads filled the arena. Following the promise . . . silence.

As I got to the parent-child relationship, I was stunned with the response. From where I stood on the speaker's platform it appeared that every man by now was on his feet, with his heart prepared to make his commitment as a dad to nurture and model strong Christian character.

I then prayed. But as I came to the end of that short prayer, the low roar returned, followed by an ever-enlarging, growing crescendo of praise. It was as if they could restrain themselves no longer. Men stood, embracing one another, shouting, applauding. The magnificent presence of the Lord suddenly turned that vast baseball stadium into a sacred place of worship. I smiled as I tried to imagine the invisible presence of angels hovering over the place where the California *Angels* play their home games. What a memory!

More importantly, think of the lives, the homes, the families that are now in the process of being changed. It all goes back to the statement I began with: The power of a promise is incredible!

May God's presence be felt in your life, and may His power enable you to keep the promises you have made.

NOTES

1. Jack Canfield and Mark Victor Hansen, *Chicken Soup for the Soul: 101 Stories to Open the Heart and Rekindle the Spirit* (Deerfield Beach, Fla.: Health Communications, Inc., 1993), 273-74.

2. Dennis Rainey, *The Tribute* (Nashville: Thomas Nelson Publishers, 1994), 3-4.

3. Randy L. Carlson, *Father Memories* (Chicago: Moody Press, 1992), 13.

4. Josiah Gilbert Holland, "God, Give Us Men," in *The Best Loved Poems of the American People*, selected by Hazel Felleman (Garden City, NY: Garden City Books, 1936), 132.